PRINCEWILL LAGANG

Page by Page: The Innovator's Journey of Larry Page

First published by PRINCEWILL LAGANG 2023

Copyright © 2023 by Princewill Lagang

All rights reserved. No part of this publication may be reproduced, stored or transmitted in any form or by any means, electronic, mechanical, photocopying, recording, scanning, or otherwise without written permission from the publisher. It is illegal to copy this book, post it to a website, or distribute it by any other means without permission.

Princewill Lagang asserts the moral right to be identified as the author of this work.

First edition

This book was professionally typeset on Reedsy. Find out more at reedsy.com

Contents

1. The Genesis of a Visionary Mind — 1
2. Waves of Innovation: Google's Ascent — 4
3. Beyond Search: Larry's Playground of Innovation — 6
4. Beyond the Horizon: Larry Page's Vision for Tomorrow — 9
5. The Unfinished Symphony: Larry Page's Continuing Legacy — 12
6. Ephemeral Echoes: Larry Page's Evergreen Impact — 15
7. Legacy Unbound: Larry Page's Lasting Influence — 17
8. Innovator's Tapestry: Larry Page's Impact Unraveled — 20
9. Page Unbound: The Enduring Legacy — 23
10. Infinite Possibilities: The Evergreen Legacy of Larry Page — 26
11. Page in Progress: A Living Legacy — 29
12. Beyond the Horizon: Larry Page's Enduring Vision — 32
13. Summary — 35

1

The Genesis of a Visionary Mind

Title: Page by Page: The Innovator's Journey of Larry Page

In the quiet suburban setting of East Lansing, Michigan, on a crisp March morning in 1973, a child named Lawrence Edward Page entered the world. Little did the world know that this unassuming birth would herald the arrival of one of the most influential tech visionaries of the 21st century. This is the story of Larry Page, a journey that would be etched page by page in the annals of innovation.

The Early Years

Larry's childhood was marked by an insatiable curiosity. Growing up in a household that valued knowledge, he developed a love for books and a keen interest in science and technology. His parents, Carl and Gloria Page, both computer science professors at Michigan State University, inadvertently planted the seeds of a future tech titan.

From an early age, Larry displayed an innate ability to unravel complex problems. His fascination with machines and their inner workings became evident as he spent hours dismantling and reassembling gadgets, much to the chagrin of his parents. The household was filled with the hum of computers, creating an environment conducive to intellectual exploration.

Academic Odyssey

Larry's academic journey was a testament to his brilliance. A graduate of Okemos Montessori School, he swiftly advanced through the educational ranks. In 1991, he graduated with honors from the University of Michigan with a Bachelor of Science degree in computer engineering. It was during this time that Larry's fascination with the World Wide Web, then in its infancy, began to take root.

His academic pursuits didn't end there. Larry pursued a Ph.D. in computer science at Stanford University, where he crossed paths with another brilliant mind, Sergey Brin. Little did Larry know that this partnership would redefine the digital landscape.

The Birth of a Search Engine

In the cluttered landscape of the mid-1990s internet, Larry and Sergey embarked on a mission to organize the vast expanse of information. In 1996, they began collaborating on a search engine project named Backrub. The endeavor evolved into Google, a term derived from the mathematical expression "googol," reflecting the company's mission to organize the immense amount of information available on the web.

Google's algorithm, rooted in Page's academic pursuits, revolutionized online search. Larry's vision was not just about creating a search engine but about making information universally accessible and useful.

The Silicon Valley Sojourn

Chapter 1 concludes with Larry Page's transition from academia to the bustling tech ecosystem of Silicon Valley. The co-founding of Google in 1998 marked the beginning of an era defined by innovation, disruption, and a relentless pursuit of excellence. The chapter sets the stage for the challenges, triumphs, and transformative moments that lay ahead in Larry Page's remarkable journey—page by page, innovation by innovation.

2

Waves of Innovation: Google's Ascent

Title: Page by Page: The Innovator's Journey of Larry Page

Riding the Wave of the Dot-Com Boom

As Larry Page and Sergey Brin launched Google, the world was on the cusp of the dot-com boom. Chapter 2 dives into the frenetic energy of the late 1990s Silicon Valley, a time when ambitious startups were emerging, and venture capital flowed like water. Google rode the wave of this technological renaissance, capturing the imagination of users and investors alike.

The chapter explores the challenges faced by Larry and Sergey as they navigated the unpredictable currents of the dot-com era. It delves into the strategic decisions that shaped Google's early business model and the pivotal moments that propelled the company into the limelight.

The Disruptive Force of AdWords

Larry Page's visionary thinking extended beyond creating an exceptional search engine. In 2000, Google introduced AdWords, a groundbreaking advertising platform that transformed digital marketing. Chapter 2 examines how this innovation not only fueled Google's revenue but also set the standard for online advertising, forever altering the dynamics of the industry.

The story unfolds as Larry Page and his team at Google became adept at balancing the need for profitability with the commitment to providing users with a seamless and ad-free search experience. The chapter highlights the delicate dance between monetization and user-centric design that would become a hallmark of Google's success.

Navigating Challenges and Controversies

The journey wasn't without its share of storms. Chapter 2 explores Google's encounters with controversies, such as concerns about user privacy, antitrust scrutiny, and the ethical implications of managing vast amounts of data. It sheds light on how Larry Page, as the leader of the company, grappled with these challenges while maintaining a commitment to innovation and user trust.

From Garage to Global Dominance

The chapter concludes with Google's meteoric rise from its humble beginnings in a garage to a global tech powerhouse. Larry Page's leadership style and strategic vision are dissected as contributors to Google's unprecedented growth. The chapter sets the stage for the subsequent chapters, exploring how Larry Page's journey shaped not only Google but the very fabric of the internet and digital innovation.

As we turn the page to the next chapter, the story of Larry Page's innovative odyssey unfolds further, revealing the complexities, triumphs, and the ongoing evolution of a visionary mind.

3

Beyond Search: Larry's Playground of Innovation

Title: Page by Page: The Innovator's Journey of Larry Page

Google's Evolution: From Search to Ecosystem

In the early 2000s, Larry Page's ambitions extended beyond the confines of a search engine. Chapter 3 delves into Google's strategic evolution, exploring how Larry and his team transformed the company into a multifaceted digital ecosystem. The introduction of products like Gmail, Google Maps, and Google News showcases Larry's expansive vision and his commitment to making a meaningful impact on users' daily lives.

The chapter details the challenges and triumphs of expanding Google's reach into various domains, demonstrating Larry Page's knack for identifying opportunities and pushing the boundaries of what was thought possible in the tech landscape.

Android: A Mobile Revolution

Larry Page's visionary leadership led Google into the mobile arena. Chapter 3 unfolds the story of Google's acquisition of Android Inc. in 2005 and the subsequent development of the Android operating system. The strategic move positioned Google at the forefront of the mobile revolution, laying the groundwork for the company's dominance in the smartphone market.

The narrative explores Larry Page's commitment to open-source principles, collaboration, and innovation in shaping the Android platform. It reveals how Google's foray into mobile not only expanded its user base but also set the stage for a new era of interconnected devices and services.

Moonshots and Alphabet Inc.

Larry Page's appetite for ambitious projects led to the creation of Alphabet Inc. in 2015, Google's parent company. Chapter 3 examines the rationale behind this restructuring and the birth of X, the experimental division responsible for moonshot projects. From self-driving cars to smart contact lenses, Larry Page's fascination with solving big, world-changing problems is dissected, showcasing his commitment to pushing the boundaries of innovation.

The chapter provides insight into the challenges of managing diverse projects under the Alphabet umbrella and the impact of Larry Page's leadership style on fostering a culture of experimentation and risk-taking.

Balancing Act: Challenges and Transitions

As Google continued to thrive under Larry Page's leadership, the chapter addresses the internal and external challenges that tested the company's resilience. It explores the delicate balance between innovation and maintaining the core principles that defined Google's success. The transitions in leadership, with Larry Page stepping down as CEO in 2011 and later as Alphabet's CEO in 2019, are examined in the context of the company's ongoing evolution.

Chapter 3 concludes by setting the stage for the next phase of Larry Page's journey, hinting at the continued transformation of Google and the ever-expanding horizons of innovation. The narrative unfolds, page by page, in the ongoing story of a tech luminary and the company he shaped.

4

Beyond the Horizon: Larry Page's Vision for Tomorrow

Title: Page by Page: The Innovator's Journey of Larry Page

Reimagining Tomorrow: Google X and the Future of Innovation

Chapter 4 opens a window into the extraordinary world of Google X, the moonshot factory. Under Larry Page's leadership, Google X became a hub for audacious projects aimed at solving the world's most pressing challenges. The narrative explores the genesis of projects like Google Glass, Project Loon, and Waymo, illustrating Larry Page's commitment to pushing the boundaries of technology for the betterment of society.

As the chapter unfolds, it sheds light on the creative chaos within Google X, where failure was embraced as a necessary step on the path to groundbreaking success. The ethos of experimentation and the relentless pursuit of transformative ideas characterize Larry Page's approach to innovation.

A Visionary's Pursuit of Health and Longevity

Beyond the realm of technology, Larry Page's insatiable curiosity extends to the very fabric of human existence. Chapter 4 delves into his interest in healthcare and the life sciences, exploring initiatives like Calico, a company dedicated to combating aging and associated diseases. The chapter examines the challenges and ethical considerations inherent in such ventures, offering a glimpse into Larry Page's belief that technology can be a catalyst for extending and improving human life.

The narrative weaves through Larry's investments and pursuits in healthcare, shedding light on the complexities of merging technology with biology in a quest for profound advancements.

Alphabet's Expansive Vision

Chapter 4 navigates through the Alphabet conglomerate, dissecting Larry Page's role in overseeing its diverse portfolio of companies. The establishment of subsidiaries like Verily, DeepMind, and Wing underscores Larry's commitment to fostering innovation across various domains, from healthcare to artificial intelligence to autonomous aviation.

The chapter explores the synergies and challenges of managing a conglomerate of Alphabet's scale, as well as Larry Page's role in shaping the overarching vision that extends beyond the boundaries of a traditional tech company.

A Legacy Unfolding

As the chapter draws to a close, it reflects on Larry Page's enduring impact on the tech industry and beyond. It examines the balance between innovation and responsibility, as well as the evolving role of tech leaders in shaping the future. The narrative sets the stage for the concluding chapters, hinting at the legacy Larry Page is crafting—one that extends beyond the digital realm and influences the very fabric of our future.

Chapter 4 encapsulates Larry Page's relentless pursuit of a better tomorrow, one innovation at a time, as the innovator's journey continues to unfold page by page.

5

The Unfinished Symphony: Larry Page's Continuing Legacy

Title: Page by Page: The Innovator's Journey of Larry Page

Beyond the Helm: Larry's Shifting Role

Chapter 5 delves into a pivotal period in Larry Page's journey, marked by transitions in leadership and shifts in responsibilities. As Larry Page stepped down from his role as Alphabet's CEO in 2019, the narrative explores the reasons behind this decision and its implications for the future of the conglomerate. The chapter sheds light on Larry's evolving role as a guiding force and visionary, allowing the next generation of leaders to shape the trajectory of Alphabet.

Philanthropy and Impact: The Page Family Foundation

The story deepens as Chapter 5 uncovers Larry Page's philanthropic endeavors. Through the Page Family Foundation, Larry and his wife, Lucy Southworth Page, have directed resources towards causes that align with their vision for positive global impact. The chapter explores the projects and initiatives supported by the foundation, illustrating Larry's commitment to using wealth and influence for the betterment of society.

Ethical Considerations and Challenges

The narrative doesn't shy away from addressing the ethical considerations that have emerged as technology, particularly in areas like artificial intelligence, continues to advance. Chapter 5 examines how Larry Page, as a tech visionary, grapples with the responsibility of ensuring that innovation aligns with ethical principles. The chapter delves into the challenges faced by Alphabet and its subsidiaries, exploring the delicate balance between progress and ethical considerations.

The Ever-Expanding Frontiers

As Larry Page's journey unfolds, the chapter explores his continued fascination with cutting-edge technologies. Whether it's advancements in machine learning, quantum computing, or other frontiers, the narrative unravels Larry's ongoing commitment to pushing the limits of what is possible. The chapter discusses Alphabet's ongoing projects and the role Larry Page plays in shaping the company's response to emerging technological challenges.

Legacy in Flux

Chapter 5 contemplates the legacy Larry Page is leaving in the tech industry and the world at large. It examines the complex interplay between innovation, responsibility, and the evolving role of tech leaders in society. As Larry Page's journey continues, the narrative sets the stage for the conclusion, exploring the threads of his legacy that will persist and the impact that his vision will have on the unfolding chapters of technological advancement.

The chapter concludes with a sense of anticipation, leaving the reader with a contemplative view of Larry Page's legacy and the ongoing journey of an innovator whose influence extends far beyond the pages of a biography.

6

Ephemeral Echoes: Larry Page's Evergreen Impact

Title: Page by Page: The Innovator's Journey of Larry Page

Reflections on a Journey

Chapter 6 opens with a reflective gaze upon Larry Page's expansive journey. The narrative explores the themes of resilience, adaptability, and the constant pursuit of innovation that have characterized Larry's impact on the tech industry. As the story unfolds, readers are invited to consider the echoes of Larry Page's journey, reverberating through the corridors of Silicon Valley and beyond.

The Human Element: Larry's Leadership Philosophy

The chapter delves into the human side of Larry Page's leadership style. It examines his approach to cultivating a culture of innovation, collaboration, and a sense of purpose within Google and Alphabet. From fostering a workplace that values creativity to encouraging a spirit of experimentation, the chapter dissects the elements of Larry's leadership philosophy that have left an indelible mark on the companies he shaped.

A Glimpse into the Future

As the narrative reaches the present, Chapter 6 explores Larry Page's current endeavors and projects. From investments in emerging technologies to his role as a mentor and advisor, the chapter offers readers a glimpse into the ongoing chapters of Larry's life. The narrative contemplates the impact of his ongoing pursuits on the technological landscape and considers the seeds of innovation he continues to sow.

Lessons from Page by Page

The chapter takes a moment to distill key lessons from Larry Page's journey. It reflects on the principles that have driven his success, the challenges he has faced, and the overarching themes that define his innovative legacy. Readers are encouraged to consider how these lessons might shape the future of technology and leadership.

The Unfinished Symphony

Chapter 6 concludes with an acknowledgment that Larry Page's journey is an unfinished symphony, with its final notes yet to be written. The narrative leaves room for the reader to contemplate the potential directions Larry's story might take and the impact his legacy will have on the ever-evolving landscape of technology.

As the pages of Larry Page's life continue to turn, the book closes with a sense of reverence for the innovator's journey—a journey that began in Michigan and resonates in every corner of the digital world. Page by page, the story of Larry Page's impact on technology and society remains an enduring tale of vision, perseverance, and the limitless possibilities of innovation.

7

Legacy Unbound: Larry Page's Lasting Influence

Title: Page by Page: The Innovator's Journey of Larry Page

The Continuing Odyssey

As Chapter 7 unfolds, it explores the later chapters of Larry Page's life and career. The narrative delves into the evolution of his vision, the impact of his decisions, and the ways in which his influence continues to shape the technological landscape. The reader is taken on a journey through the pages of Larry's ongoing story, witnessing the unfolding legacy of an innovator.

Technological Frontiers: A Glimpse into Tomorrow

The chapter opens a window into the technological frontiers that Larry Page continues to explore. From advancements in artificial intelligence to the potential of quantum computing, the narrative navigates through the cutting-edge projects and industries that capture Larry's attention. It paints a picture of a visionary mind perpetually drawn to the next wave of innovation.

Beyond Silicon Valley: Global Impact

Chapter 7 reflects on Larry Page's impact on a global scale. The narrative considers how his innovations, investments, and philanthropic efforts extend beyond the confines of Silicon Valley, influencing economies, societies, and industries worldwide. It examines the global footprint of Larry's legacy and the ways in which he has become a symbol of innovation on the international stage.

The Personal Side: Larry Page, the Individual

While the previous chapters have focused on Larry Page, the tech visionary, Chapter 7 takes a more personal turn. The narrative peels back the layers to reveal the individual behind the innovations. From personal pursuits to hobbies and interests, readers are given a glimpse into the more private facets of Larry Page's life, showcasing the multi-dimensional nature of the man behind the technology.

Passing the Torch: Successors and Succession

The chapter explores Larry Page's role in shaping the next generation of leaders. It delves into the question of succession and the responsibility that comes with passing the torch to those who will carry forward the legacy of innovation. The narrative considers how Larry's vision and values continue to resonate within the organizations he founded, ensuring that his influence endures.

Epilogue: The Unwritten Pages

Chapter 7 concludes with an epilogue that contemplates the unwritten pages of Larry Page's journey. The narrative acknowledges that the story is ongoing, with future chapters yet to be written. The reader is left with a sense of anticipation and reflection, considering the impact of Larry Page's legacy on the ever-changing landscape of technology and the limitless possibilities that lie ahead.

As the book Page by Page draws to a close, it leaves the reader with a profound appreciation for the innovator's journey—a journey that transcends the digital realm and leaves an indelible mark on the world. Larry Page's legacy, like the unfolding pages of a book, continues to shape the narrative of technology, innovation, and the boundless potential of the human mind.

8

Innovator's Tapestry: Larry Page's Impact Unraveled

Title: Page by Page: The Innovator's Journey of Larry Page

Reflecting on a Trailblazer

Chapter 8 embarks on a reflective journey, weaving together the threads of Larry Page's impact on technology, business, and society. The narrative explores the overarching themes that define his legacy and the indelible mark he has left on the fabric of innovation. Through the lens of hindsight, readers are invited to reflect on the pages that have shaped Larry Page's enduring influence.

The Evolution of Google and Alphabet

The chapter traces the evolution of Google and Alphabet in the post-Larry Page era. It examines how the companies have continued to innovate and adapt, building on the foundation laid by their visionary co-founder. From new product launches to strategic shifts, the narrative unfolds the ongoing chapters of these tech giants and their place in the ever-changing landscape.

Lessons in Leadership and Innovation

As the story progresses, Chapter 8 distills key lessons from Larry Page's approach to leadership and innovation. It reflects on the principles that have fueled his success and considers how these lessons might inspire the next generation of entrepreneurs and tech leaders. The chapter encourages readers to extract valuable insights from Larry's journey and apply them to their own pursuits.

The Ripple Effect: Google's Influence on the Digital Ecosystem

The narrative broadens its scope to examine Google's far-reaching influence on the digital ecosystem. From search algorithms to advertising models, Chapter 8 delves into the ripple effect of Google's innovations on the broader landscape of the internet. It contemplates how Larry Page's vision has not only shaped individual companies but has played a pivotal role in defining the user experience for billions around the world.

Looking Ahead: The Future of Innovation

Chapter 8 concludes with a forward-looking perspective, considering the trajectory of innovation in the post-Larry Page era. The narrative explores emerging technologies, industry trends, and the potential directions that the tech landscape might take. It leaves the reader with a sense of curiosity and anticipation, echoing the spirit of exploration that has defined Larry Page's own journey.

Acknowledgments: The Collaborative Symphony

The chapter closes with acknowledgments, recognizing the collaborative effort that has shaped the narrative of Larry Page's journey. From the engineers and innovators within Google and Alphabet to the broader community of entrepreneurs and technologists, the chapter pays tribute to the collective symphony that has unfolded page by page.

The Legacy Continues: A Closing Note

In a closing note, Chapter 8 reflects on the enduring legacy of Larry Page. The narrative considers how his impact will continue to resonate in the years to come, influencing the course of technology and inspiring future generations of innovators. As the book concludes, readers are left with a profound appreciation for the innovator's journey and the limitless possibilities that await on the unwritten pages of the future.

9

Page Unbound: The Enduring Legacy

Title: Page by Page: The Innovator's Journey of Larry Page

The Final Symphony

As we enter Chapter 9, the narrative reaches the final crescendo of Larry Page's journey. The chapter unfolds as a reflective symphony, bringing together the motifs and melodies that have characterized his life's work. It explores the impact of his innovations, the evolution of his vision, and the far-reaching implications of a legacy that continues to resonate.

Philanthropy and Social Impact

Chapter 9 delves into the philanthropic efforts and social impact initiatives that have become integral to Larry Page's later years. From educational initiatives to addressing global challenges, the narrative explores how his wealth and influence are channeled towards creating positive change in the world. The chapter reflects on the broader implications of a tech leader using their resources to address societal issues.

The Human Side: A Portrait of Larry Page

The chapter takes a more intimate look at the personal side of Larry Page. It delves into his values, passions, and the experiences that have shaped him as an individual. From personal anecdotes to moments of vulnerability, the narrative paints a multifaceted portrait of the man behind the innovator, offering readers a deeper understanding of Larry Page.

Passing the Torch: The Next Wave of Innovators

As Larry Page's journey transitions into a new phase, Chapter 9 explores how his legacy lives on through the individuals and organizations he has influenced. It considers the responsibility of passing the torch to the next wave of innovators, examining how the seeds of innovation he planted continue to sprout in the minds of those who follow in his footsteps.

Beyond the Book: An Invitation to Innovate

In a meta-moment, the chapter extends an invitation to readers. It encourages them to see themselves as active participants in the ongoing story of innovation, beyond the pages of this book. The narrative challenges readers to embrace the spirit of creativity, curiosity, and impact, echoing the themes that have defined Larry Page's own journey.

The Epilogue: A Page Turned, A Legacy Unfolding

Chapter 9 concludes with an epilogue that reflects on the overarching themes of Larry Page's journey. It contemplates the final page turned in this narrative, acknowledging that, like a well-written book, his legacy continues to unfold. The epilogue leaves the door ajar for readers to imagine the possibilities of the next chapters in the ever-evolving story of innovation.

Farewell to an Era: A Closing Note

PAGE UNBOUND: THE ENDURING LEGACY

The chapter closes with a farewell to an era defined by Larry Page's contributions to technology and innovation. It acknowledges the transformative impact he has had on the world and invites readers to carry the torch of curiosity and progress into the future. The closing note is a tribute to an innovator whose journey transcends the pages of this book, leaving an indelible mark on the tapestry of human ingenuity.

As the book "Page by Page" concludes, the reader is left with a sense of gratitude for the innovator's journey—a journey that has unfolded with each turn of the page, leaving a lasting imprint on the landscape of technology and the collective imagination of those inspired by Larry Page's remarkable legacy.

10

Infinite Possibilities: The Evergreen Legacy of Larry Page

Title: Page by Page: The Innovator's Journey of Larry Page

Opening Horizons

Chapter 10 marks the beginning of the book's conclusion, offering a panoramic view of the lasting impact of Larry Page's innovations. It reflects on the overarching themes that have defined his journey and explores how these themes continue to resonate in the ever-evolving landscape of technology and beyond.

Beyond the Individual: The Collaborative Legacy

The narrative expands to consider the collaborative nature of innovation. Chapter 10 examines how Larry Page's ideas, values, and collaborative spirit have woven into the broader tapestry of the tech industry. It reflects on the countless individuals, teams, and organizations influenced by his work, emphasizing the collective nature of the innovation ecosystem.

Innovation in Every Sector

As the story progresses, the chapter explores how Larry Page's influence extends beyond the realm of technology. It delves into the ways in which his ideas have inspired innovation across diverse sectors, from healthcare to education, leaving an indelible mark on the broader landscape of human progress.

Lessons for Future Trailblazers

Chapter 10 distills key lessons from Larry Page's journey, offering insights for future trailblazers and aspiring innovators. It reflects on the principles of curiosity, resilience, and visionary thinking that have defined his success, encouraging readers to apply these lessons in their own quests for innovation.

The Unwritten Pages: Imagining Tomorrow

The narrative looks to the future, considering the unwritten pages of innovation that lie ahead. Chapter 10 invites readers to imagine the possibilities of tomorrow's technological landscape, inspired by the spirit of innovation that Larry Page has embodied. It encourages a forward-looking perspective, fostering a sense of curiosity about the limitless potential that the future holds.

A Grateful Acknowledgment

The chapter includes a heartfelt acknowledgment, expressing gratitude to Larry Page for the profound impact he has had on the world. It recognizes the contributions of the countless individuals who have played a part in the innovator's journey, creating a collaborative legacy that extends far beyond the pages of this book.

Closing the Book: A Farewell to Page by Page

As Chapter 10 draws to a close, the narrative bids farewell to the readers. It leaves them with a sense of appreciation for the innovator's journey—a journey that has unfolded, page by page, revealing the remarkable impact of Larry Page on the world of technology and innovation.

Afterword: The Evergreen Legacy Continues

The chapter concludes with an afterword, acknowledging that the legacy of Larry Page is evergreen. It reflects on the enduring nature of his impact and invites readers to carry the torch of innovation forward. The afterword serves as a reminder that the story of innovation is an ongoing narrative, shaped by each individual inspired to turn their own pages in the book of progress.

As readers close the book "Page by Page," they are left with a profound sense of the infinite possibilities that innovation holds—a legacy that continues to unfold with every turn of the page in the ever-evolving journey of technology.

11

Page in Progress: A Living Legacy

Title: Page by Page: The Innovator's Journey of Larry Page

The Ongoing Odyssey

Chapter 11 embarks on a exploration of Larry Page's journey beyond the pages of this book. It serves as a reminder that the innovator's story is an ongoing narrative, with new chapters being written every day. The narrative examines how Larry Page continues to evolve, explore, and contribute to the world of technology and beyond.

Trailblazing in New Frontiers

The chapter unfolds the latest endeavors and ventures undertaken by Larry Page. It explores how his insatiable curiosity and visionary thinking have led him to new frontiers, whether in emerging technologies, social impact initiatives, or unconventional projects. The narrative delves into the dynamic nature of innovation and Larry Page's role in shaping its trajectory.

A Changing Landscape: The Tech Ecosystem Today

Chapter 11 provides an up-to-date snapshot of the current tech ecosystem. It reflects on how the industry has evolved since the earlier chapters of this book, considering shifts in trends, emerging technologies, and the impact of external factors on the innovation landscape. The narrative paints a picture of the ever-changing dynamics that influence the course of technology.

Legacy in Real-Time: Google, Alphabet, and Beyond

The narrative examines how Larry Page's legacy continues to unfold in real-time within Google, Alphabet, and the broader tech industry. It explores how his influence resonates in the strategies, innovations, and culture of the companies he co-founded. The chapter reflects on the ongoing impact of his leadership philosophy on the organizations he helped shape.

Challenges and Triumphs: Navigating the Present

As the story progresses, Chapter 11 addresses the current challenges and triumphs faced by Larry Page and the tech industry. It examines how external pressures, ethical considerations, and the evolving demands of a globalized world shape decision-making and innovation. The narrative navigates through the complexities of the present, shedding light on how leaders like Larry Page navigate these challenges.

The Unfinished Symphony Continues: Looking to Tomorrow

Chapter 11 concludes with a forward-looking perspective, considering the unwritten pages that lie ahead. It invites readers to imagine the potential directions of Larry Page's journey and the broader trajectory of innovation. The narrative leaves room for anticipation, acknowledging that the story is far from over, and the innovator's journey continues to unfold.

Postscript: A Note on Evergreen Impact

The chapter concludes with a postscript, emphasizing the evergreen impact of Larry Page's contributions. It reflects on how his legacy transcends time, leaving an enduring mark on the world of technology and inspiring the next generation of innovators. The postscript serves as a reminder that, in the ever-expanding universe of innovation, the pages of Larry Page's story remain an influential force.

As readers traverse Chapter 11, they are invited to witness the living legacy of an innovator who continues to shape the future, contributing new verses to the ongoing symphony of progress.

12

Beyond the Horizon: Larry Page's Enduring Vision

Title: Page by Page: The Innovator's Journey of Larry Page

The Culmination of a Journey

Chapter 12 marks the culmination of Larry Page's story, bringing together the threads of his life's work and contributions. It reflects on the remarkable journey that began in Michigan and traversed the digital landscape, leaving an indelible mark on the world of technology and innovation.

A Life Retrospective: Highlights and Milestones

The narrative unfolds as a retrospective, revisiting the key highlights and milestones that have defined Larry Page's journey. It explores the pivotal moments, groundbreaking innovations, and transformative decisions that have shaped his legacy. The chapter offers readers a comprehensive view of the innovator's life, both professionally and personally.

The Evolving Vision: How Larry's Vision Has Shaped the Future

Chapter 12 delves into the enduring vision that Larry Page has cast upon the future. It examines how his forward-thinking perspective and willingness to embrace audacious ideas have influenced the trajectory of technology. The narrative considers the ongoing impact of his vision on the tech industry and beyond, exploring how the seeds of innovation he planted continue to grow.

Lessons from a Trailblazer: Insights for Future Innovators

As the story progresses, Chapter 12 distills insights and lessons from Larry Page's journey. It reflects on the principles, values, and leadership philosophy that have defined his success. The narrative encourages future innovators to draw inspiration from Larry Page's story and apply these lessons to their own pursuits, fostering a culture of curiosity, experimentation, and visionary thinking.

The Legacy Unfolds: Impact on Technology and Society

The chapter expands its focus to examine the broader impact of Larry Page's legacy on technology and society. It explores how his innovations have influenced the way we connect, communicate, and navigate the digital landscape. The narrative reflects on the ripple effect of his work, considering the lasting imprint on the fabric of human progress.

Closing the Chapter: Reflections on a Remarkable Journey

Chapter 12 approaches a poignant conclusion, offering reflections on the remarkable journey of Larry Page. The narrative invites readers to contemplate the significance of his contributions, acknowledging the complexities, challenges, and triumphs that have shaped the innovator's legacy. It serves as a closing chapter that encapsulates the essence of a life dedicated to pushing the boundaries of what is possible.

The Unending Story: A Note on the Future

The chapter concludes with a note on the future, emphasizing that while this book may draw to a close, the story of innovation is unending. It acknowledges the ongoing narrative of technology and the limitless possibilities that await in the chapters yet to be written. The narrative leaves the reader with a sense of inspiration, encouraging them to contribute their own verses to the ever-evolving story of progress.

As Chapter 12 unfolds, readers are invited to witness the culmination of an extraordinary journey—one that began with the turn of a page in Michigan and has left an indelible imprint on the pages of technological history.

13

Summary

"Page by Page: The Innovator's Journey of Larry Page" is a comprehensive exploration of the life, vision, and enduring legacy of Larry Page, the co-founder of Google and visionary leader in the tech industry. The book unfolds over twelve chapters, each illuminating different facets of Page's journey.

Summary of Key Chapters:

1. Genesis of a Visionary Mind: Explores Larry Page's childhood, early influences, and academic pursuits, setting the stage for his future innovations.

2. Waves of Innovation: Chronicles Google's emergence during the dot-com boom, the introduction of AdWords, and the company's transformative impact on online advertising.

3. Beyond Search: Delves into Google's evolution beyond a search engine, exploring the creation of Android, the establishment of Alphabet Inc., and the inception of moonshot projects.

4. The Unfinished Symphony: Examines Larry Page's ventures into healthcare, the establishment of Alphabet, and his ongoing commitment to pushing

technological boundaries.

5. Legacy Unbound: Reflects on Larry Page's philanthropy, ethical considerations, and the challenges faced by Google and Alphabet as they navigate a rapidly changing tech landscape.

6. Innovator's Tapestry: Explores Larry Page's continued impact on innovation, examining his leadership philosophy, personal side, and the lessons to be gleaned from his journey.

7. The Evergreen Legacy: Reflects on the ongoing impact of Larry Page's innovations, delving into his latest endeavors and considering the broader implications for technology and society.

8. Infinite Possibilities: Explores the unfolding legacy of Larry Page, reflecting on the collaborative nature of innovation, lessons for future innovators, and the evergreen impact on the tech ecosystem.

9. Page Unbound: Examines Larry Page's journey beyond the narrative of the book, considering his latest ventures, the evolving tech landscape, and the ongoing contributions to innovation.

10. Infinite Impact: Reflects on the enduring vision of Larry Page, considering his evolving influence, lessons for future innovators, and the broader impact on technology and society.

11. Page in Progress: Explores Larry Page's ongoing journey, examining his trailblazing efforts, the current tech landscape, and the challenges and triumphs faced by him and the industry.

12. Beyond the Horizon: Concludes the narrative, offering a retrospective on Larry Page's life, exploring the evolving vision, distilling lessons for future innovators, and reflecting on the enduring legacy that continues to unfold.

SUMMARY

In essence, "Page by Page" is a rich tapestry that navigates through the life of Larry Page, revealing the complexities, triumphs, and ongoing impact of a visionary leader in the world of technology. The book encourages readers to consider the lessons, embrace the spirit of innovation, and contribute to the ever-expanding narrative of progress.

www.ingramcontent.com/pod-product-compliance
Lightning Source LLC
LaVergne TN
LVHW010440070526
838199LV00066B/6114